The Illustrated Story of President

SPENCER W. KIMBALL

Great Leaders of The Church
of Jesus Christ of Latter-day Saints

The Illustrated Story of President Spencer W. Kimball
Great Leaders of The Church of Jesus Christ
of Latter-day Saints

Copyright © 1982 by
Eagle Systems International
P.O. Box 508
Provo, Utah 84603

ISBN: 0-938762-12-5
Library of Congress Catalog Card No.: 82-71683

Fourth Printing April 1987

First Edition

Lithographed in U.S.A.
by
COMMUNITY PRESS, INC.

A Member of
The American Bookseller's Association
New York, New York

The Illustrated Story of President

SPENCER W. KIMBALL

Great Leaders of The Church
of Jesus Christ of Latter-day Saints

We thank the family of Spencer W. Kimball for their generous help and cooperation in this project.

AUTHOR
Della Mae Rasmussen

ILLUSTRATOR
B. Keith Christensen

DIRECTOR AND CORRELATOR
Lael J. Woodbury

ADVISORS AND EDITORS

Paul & Millie Cheesman
Mark Ray Davis
L. Norman Egan
Annette Hullinger
Beatrice W. Friel
Kathy Grant

PUBLISHER
Steven R. Shallenberger

A
Biography Of
SPENCER W. KIMBALL

Spencer W. Kimball, twelfth president and prophet of The Church of Jesus Christ of Latter-day Saints, was born in Salt Lake City, Utah, on March 28, 1895, to Andrew and Olive Woolley Kimball. Spencer was the sixth child in the family. When Spencer was three years old, his father moved the family to Thatcher, Arizona, where he was called to be president of the St. Joseph Stake.

Spencer lived a full and happy childhood in Thatcher. He worked on the family farm, excelled in school, and fulfilled both Church and school leadership positions. He was a conscientious boy and always tried to do his best in any assignment.

Spencer graduated from Gila Academy with highest honors in 1914. Soon after this he received a mission call to the Swiss-German Mission, but because of the outbreak of World War I, his assignment was changed to the Central States Mission. When he returned from his mission, he attended the University of Arizona and then Brigham Young University in Provo, Utah, for a time.

He married Camilla Eyring on November 16, 1917. They were sealed in the Salt Lake temple in June, 1918.

Early in 1918 he was called as a stake clerk, serving under his father, who was stake president. At the death of his father in 1924 Spencer was named second counselor in the St. Joseph stake presidency, and in 1938 he was called to be president of the newly organized Mt. Graham Stake.

Spencer was a successful businessman, being half-owner and manager of an insurance and realty company. In addition he was a member of numerous town boards and committees.

On October 7, 1943, Spencer W. Kimball was ordained a member of the Council of the Twelve Apostles. He served with dedication as an apostle for thirty years.

He suffered health problems but always asked for and received strength from the Lord to fulfill his callings. He lost most of his vocal cords in cancer surgery in 1957, and in 1972 he underwent open-heart surgery.

Spencer W. Kimball was sustained president of the Church on December 30, 1973. His administration was one of growth and accomplishment for the Church. He toured the world, visiting the Saints and presiding over area conferences. New temples were announced worldwide. Missionary work experienced tremendous growth. He implemented the consolidated meeting schedule to allow families more time to be together and study the gospel. He was well-known for his powerful talks to the Saints stressing morality, modesty, repentance, missionary work, and building eternal marriages. His book *The Miracle of Forgiveness* has been a source of help to thousands of people. The Lord revealed through President Kimball that the priesthood should be extended to all worthy male members of the Church.

Spencer W. Kimball passed away quietly in his sleep on November 5, 1985, at the age of 90. He had served as president of the Church almost 13 years. He was a man characterized by humility, compassion, intelligence, and total dedication to the Lord. He remains beloved by the Latter-day Saints as a mighty man of God.

"It's a nine-pound boy!" This happy announcement marked the beginning of a remarkable life—that of Spencer Woolley Kimball. The birth took place on March 28, 1895, in Salt Lake City. The baby's parents, Andrew and Olive Woolley Kimball, were proud of their son, the sixth child in the family. The only one who did not seem delighted was his ten-year-old sister, Clare. Andrew Kimball wrote, "I took the children in to see the new baby. Clare had made up her mind for a girl, was badly disappointed, and had a crying spell." Clare's feelings couldn't help but change because Spencer was a particularly handsome and bright little boy.

The Kimball family lived in Salt Lake City until Spencer was three years old. Then his father, Andrew Kimball, was called to be a stake president in Arizona, and the family moved to Thatcher, Arizona.

From the beginning it was apparent that Spencer was no ordinary child. His father once said to a neighbor, "That boy, Spencer, is an exceptional boy. He always tries to mind me, whatever I ask him to do. . . . I have dedicated him to the service of God, and he will become a mighty man in the Church."

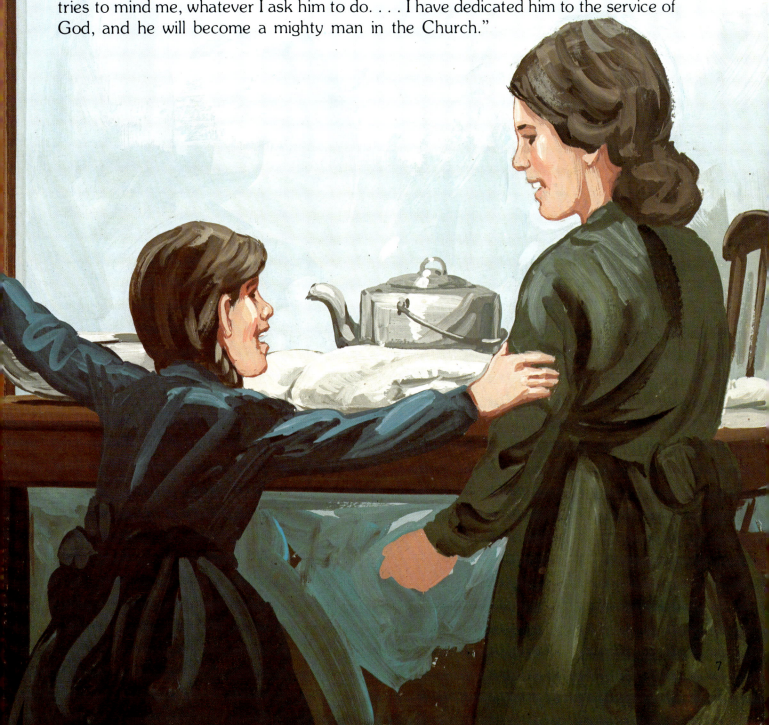

It was true. Spencer, as a boy, gave promise of becoming a mighty man in the Church. For one thing, he seemed to have something inside of him that urged him to excel and always do his best. For instance, how many nine-year-old boys decide on their own to study and memorize scriptures and Church hymns? Well, Spencer did just that. Spencer had chores to do on the farm, and his duty was to milk nine cows every morning and evening. Now milking cows isn't one of the most exciting things a person can do, but Spencer figured out a way to make good use of the time. He decided, "This is one place I can find peace and quiet to memorize. I could write down things I need to learn on a paper and put it where I can read it while I milk the cows." In this way Spencer learned the Articles of Faith, the Ten Commandments, and many of the hymns. He sang the Church songs to the cows at the top of his lungs. They must surely have been the most religious animals in the state of Arizona!

Milking was not Spencer's only chore. There was always work to be done on the farm—feeding the pigs, watering the horses, herding the cows, and cleaning the yard. Arizona was mostly hot and dry, and for Andrew and Olive Kimball it was not easy to support their growing family. Spencer wore hand-me-down sweaters, coats, and shirts made by his mother. Father, mother, brothers, and sisters all worked hard together. They had what they needed but not a penny to waste. Spencer knew a boy in Thatcher whose father owned the ice cream parlor. Sometimes Spencer watched as the boy ate a free dish of ice cream or a stick of candy. He must have wished for a few extra pennies just then!

Even so, life was not all hard work and going without new clothes and a dish of ice cream. No, indeed! Spencer thought the small desert town of Thatcher was the best possible place for a boy to grow up. He was a fun-loving youngster and had many friends. The boys and girls would call, "Come on, let's play kick-the-can!" And away Spencer would run to join in the fun. They played games like pom-pom-pull-away and pop-the-whip, too. His mother would sometimes sigh and shake her head when he ran in from play with his pants torn and his knees scraped. Once in awhile, like most boys, he had a fight. He usually came out all right, though, because he could outwrestle almost any boy that was near his size. He said later with a little note of pride, "I was tough and strong . . . I was pretty husky." For the most part he had the kindest heart, even as a very young boy. He would come to the rescue of anyone who was hurt.

One day when Spencer was about seven, he had a frightening experience. A group of families went swimming together. Spencer's father took Spencer up on his back for a ride around the pond. Spencer was afraid of the deep water. He thought, "Father is such a good swimmer. I wish I could swim like he does." Then he panicked, "Take me back, take me back, Pa!" Spencer took one step toward shore and fell into a deep hole. Down, down, he sank into the water—it filled his lungs! He tried to scream. Finally someone noticed his struggles and called for help. His father came running to pull him out. Spencer was full of water, choking, coughing, and crying. He thought he had drowned! When it was all over, he said to himself, "I was saved from drowning. The Lord must have something for me to do."

Even if Andrew and Olive Kimball had known they were preparing their son to become a prophet of God, they could not have been better teachers. Andrew served with complete devotion as stake president, and Olive supported him in every way. The family always attended church together. They knelt before meals to pray. Spencer's nightly prayers were said at his mother's knee. The family fasted together and constantly asked the Lord for protection and guidance. The parents taught their children gospel principles. Olive Kimball said to her son, "Spencer, count out the eggs for our tithing. One egg for Heavenly Father, nine eggs for the family." Andrew said to his sons, "The best hay is on the west side of the field. Get your load for the tithing barn from that side and load it full and high." The boys learned that only the best was good enough for the Lord.

Spencer always went to Primary. He was so faithful that his older brothers would tease and say things like, "There goes Spencer off to Primary. He figures it's a good way to get out of work!"

Spencer was president of his deacon's quorum and was called to other leadership positions during his youth. The principles of the gospel influenced all of his decisions. Even though he was a fun-loving boy, he could not join in when the crowd went stealing melons. He said, "It is not fair that the farmer should work so hard to raise his crop and then have it stolen or spoiled." In the same way, he would not join in Halloween pranks. He was remarkably concerned and thoughtful of others.

When he was very young, Spencer made an important decision. He said to himself, "I am going to try to live every commandment. I will not smoke or drink or break the commandments. I will decide once and then I will not have to decide again." So he never tried smoking or drinking or other bad habits.

It was clear very early that Spencer was an intelligent boy. He always did his schoolwork well. He was only ten years old when he began to help with his father's letters. Spencer made up his own system of shorthand and taught himself to type with two fingers. He liked to help his father and he was proud to be asked to do the work.

Spencer was only eleven years old when his mother died. It was a very sad time for the young boy. He loved his mother dearly and was very close to her. He missed her more than anyone could know. Later his father married a fine lady, who became mother to the Kimball children. They called her "Aunt Josie."

One day there was great excitement! Spencer's father had bought one of the first pianos in the whole area. Spencer was delighted. "I want to learn to play the piano, Father!" So his father arranged for him to have lessons. However, the excitement began to wear off when he had to practice! Still, Andrew was determined that Spencer should learn to play, so he said, "You may be excused from some of the chores if you practice your piano lesson, Spencer." So Spencer practiced! His older brothers, Gordon and Del, half-jokingly said something like, "You always want to practice when it is the hottest outside," or "There's Spencer—you can bet he'll be practicing the old piano if there's plowing and weeding to do!" Spencer *did* learn to play the piano. Eventually he played so well that some friends asked him to join an orchestra and play for dances in the area. He also enjoyed getting his friends together to sing around the piano. He probably thought to himself, "It is a lot of fun to sing and play. I'm glad I kept practicing after all!"

Spencer and his friends had many good times together. Besides singing around the piano and going to dances, they often went out into the desert for corn roasts or watermelon busts. They rode hayracks up into the nearby canyon for swimming and picnics.

When Spencer entered Gila Academy for high school, he was about the youngest in the class, but his leadership qualities were recognized anyway. Soon after school began, the freshman class met to elect a president. One girl called out, "Mr. Chairman, I make an *emotion* that we elect Spencer Kimball as our class president." Even though she got her "emotions" and her "motions" mixed up, another shouted, "Mr. Chairman, I close the ballot." Everyone looked at each other. They did not know what to do next, so Spencer became president. Not only that, but he was reelected president all three of his next years in high school. As usual he excelled in his studies. Spencer could also hold his own in athletics. He never grew to be large in size, but he was quick and full of grit and determination. He went into athletics with his usual tremendous energy. One day the Thatcher track team was competing in a meet in Mesa. They had lost most of the events when the mile race came up. The coach looked at the boys. Most of them had already run in the sprint events, and they were exhausted. Spencer was the only one rested. "Spencer," said the coach, "I guess we'll let you run in the mile." Spencer marched up to the starting line in his overalls and tennis shoes. He had never run the mile before. The signal was given and away he went. The other boys had trained for the mile and were soon ahead of him. He would not give up. He thought, "I would rather die than quit." Perhaps he thought he would die! He ran on and on, thinking, "Will it never end?" The end of the race was a blur; he fell across the line. His friends patted him on the back. Someone said, "Well, Spencer, you came in third anyway." This was small cause for celebration. There were only three running in the race!

Basketball was Spencer's great love—everything else took second place. He was the smallest boy in the class, but he was quick and could send the ball swishing through the basket. He couldn't get enough of the game. The team practiced every afternoon, and Spencer forgot all

about time when he was playing basketball. He had milking to do, but he stayed at practice until the last minute. Then he ran home as fast as he could. Aunt Josie would scold a little, "Spencer, not again! You're late every night, and the neighbor boys have to wait for their milk. You don't remember a thing when you get to playing basketball! Just like a boy!"

23

In the spring of 1914 Spencer graduated from Gila Academy with highest scholastic honors. He and his friends talked about their plans. Spencer decided that he would go to the University of Arizona in the fall. At graduation Spencer, as class president, gave a talk. He also was in a quartet and sang a baritone solo. People in the audience probably thought, "Now there is a man of many talents!" Then it was time for Andrew Kimball, as president of the school board, to give a speech. Suddenly Spencer sat straight up. His father had just announced, "Spencer will not be going to the University of Arizona in the fall. He will be serving a mission for the Church!" One of Spencer's classmates saw his face. She thought, "It looks as if Spencer is going to pass out." But he didn't, and of course he began to prepare for his mission with his usual energy.

It was the third summer he had worked at a dairy in a nearby town, but this summer he had a special goal. He earned $62.50 a month, plus his meals and a bed. He paid his tithing and set aside a little money for a nickel ice cream cone and an occasional chocolate candy bar. The rest he saved for his mission. The work at the dairy was hard. With the other hired boys, he worked from eight o'clock in the morning until two a.m. the following morning. He fed and milked cows, washed bottles, cared for the calves, and cleaned up the barn. Sometimes his fingers would be so dry and tender from the work that they would swell up, crack, and bleed. One Sunday he and some of the other boys were walking into town to go to Sunday School. They held their hands high over their heads so the swelling would hurt less. Spencer was always ready with a joke. "People who see us will think we are giving up and surrendering!" he said with a chuckle. So the boys laughed and put their hands into their pockets whenever they passed anyone.

When the summer ended, Spencer's boss, a non-Mormon, had a farewell party and gave Spencer a fine gold watch. Spencer was pleased and asked, "How could you do so much for me?" Then he climbed onto the train heading for Thatcher. When the train pulled into the station, his friends were there to greet him. They had planned parties, dances, and picnics for the weeks until he left on his mission. He was loved by his friends. One of them said, "Spencer is always the life of the party." Another said, "He has a jolly laugh that keeps everyone else laughing!"

Spencer was first called to the Swiss-German Mission, but with the outbreak of World War I his assignment was changed to the Central States Mission. In October, 1914, Spencer once again climbed onto the train. He was excited to serve a mission, but he was a little sad as he waved good-bye to his old friends. Perhaps he realized that his boyhood was past and that life would never be the same again.

With his usual enthusiasm and determination to do his best, Spencer began his mission. He studied, preached, knocked on doors, and walked miles and miles through the towns and the countryside.

One day he was especially happy he had learned to play the piano. Spencer and his companion were talking to a lady at her home. She was just going to close her door when Spencer noticed a piano in her living room. He said, "You have a nice looking piano."

"We just bought it," said the woman.

"It's a Kimball, isn't it? That's my name, too. I can play a song on it for you that you might like to hear."

The lady was surprised but answered, "Surely, come in."

Spencer played and sang the song O, *My Father*.

Perhaps the lady never joined the Church, but she could not have helped but be impressed by the sincere young missionary who bore his testimony through song.

Spencer's faith and testimony grew stronger during his mission. One day when he and his companion had hardly a penny left in their pockets, they prayed to the Lord that they would have help. Soon after, a letter arrived from one of his friends at the dairy. The boy smoked and did not attend Church, but in the letter he sent two dollars to help Spencer on his mission. Spencer was surprised and very relieved. He said, "That is the most welcome two dollars I have ever seen in my life!"

THINK ABOUT IT:

1. Tell about some of the interesting experiences Spencer had as a youth that show the kind of a person he was growing to be.
2. How did Spencer earn money for his mission?

29

In 1917 when Spencer returned to Thatcher after his mission, he found things changed. Some of his family had married and moved away. Many of his friends were attending college or had married. He sometimes felt lonely. Then one day he noticed in the newspaper an article about a new teacher at Gila Academy, a Miss Camilla Eyring. He remembered he had met her at a dance just before his mission. He said aloud to himself, "There's my wife. I am going to marry her." He lost no time in meeting Camilla. They dated that summer, and he missed her very much when he left Thatcher to attend school at BYU in Provo, Utah. When he returned home, he asked her to marry him, which she did on November 16, 1917.

Spencer went to work on farms in the area, digging ditches, harvesting crops, and irrigating. He earned two dollars a day. Then he was offered a job in the local bank, earning seventy-five dollars a month. With some of his first money he bought Camilla a wedding ring for seven dollars. The young couple saved every penny they could, and in June of 1918 they traveled to Salt Lake City to be sealed in the temple there. In the next years they became the parents of four outstanding children, Olive Beth, Spencer LeVan, Andrew Eyring, and Edward Lawrence.

Spencer's father had been a stake president for many years and in early 1918 he called Spencer to be his stake clerk. He served for six and one half years in this position. When Andrew Kimball died, President Heber J. Grant called Spencer to be a counselor in the new stake presidency. Spencer was still in his twenties, but he gladly accepted the call. He knew his Heavenly Father would help him.

Eventually a new stake, Mt. Graham, was created. Spencer W. Kimball became its first president. Spencer's older brothers said to President Grant, "Spencer is a young man. Such a big job will make an old man of him before his time." President Grant answered, "Spencer has been called to this work, and he can do as he pleases about it." Spencer, of course, would not think of refusing the call. He simply said humbly, "I hope I will be equal to the task. I promise the Lord I will do my best."

How he worked! He knew personally almost every person, adult or child, in the Gila Valley. He spent time with the sick, he performed weddings, he gave talks, and he counseled those who were troubled.

One Sunday he visited a ward in a nearby town. As he sat on the stand, he noticed five young boys sitting on the front row. They were all crossing their legs, putting their hands to their faces, uncrossing their legs, and scratching their sides. Suddenly he realized, "Why, they are copying my every movement! This is a lesson to me that I must be an example at all times. I must be careful of my actions!"

Besides his attention to the Church and his family, Spencer became a city and business leader as well. He was half-owner and manager of an insurance and real estate company. He bought a small farm. He served on various town boards and committees. Spencer was recognized for his intelligence, his dedication to his assignments, and his habit of always doing his best. When a newspaper asked its readers, who was the most prominent man in the Gila Valley, Spencer Kimball was named the man.

36

Thus the years went by. Spencer and Camilla built their dream home in Safford, Arizona, and celebrated their twenty-fifth wedding anniversary. Camilla must have thought, "We have our lovely, new home, just as I have always wanted, and we have a wonderful life here with our family and friends and our Church." It seemed as if they were settled for the rest of their lives.

However, tremendous changes were about to take place. In April, 1943, Spencer went to Salt Lake City for general conference. He felt honored when he was asked to open one of the sessions with prayer. Later he was invited into the homes of several general authorities. Spencer thought they were very friendly and again felt honored. He did not realize that they were taking a close look at him with a great calling in mind!

Spencer's cousin, Preston Parkinson, took Spencer to his hotel after conference. Preston said, "If you move to Salt Lake City, they will make an apostle out of you." Spencer answered, "Preston, that's silly. They would never pick me, with all the great men in the Church."

Back in Arizona, Spencer went about his usual work. One day he went home for lunch. As he entered the house, he heard his young son, Eddie, say "No, Daddy is not here . . . oh, yes . . . here he comes."

"Daddy," said Eddie, "Salt Lake City is calling." Spencer took the phone.

"Spencer, this is Brother Clark. Do you have a chair handy?"

40

It was the voice of President J. Reuben Clark, first counselor in the First Presidency. President Clark continued, "Spencer, the Brethren have just chosen you to fill one of the vacancies in the Quorum of the Twelve."

Spencer could not believe his own ears. When he found his voice, he stammered, "Oh, Brother Clark! Not me! You don't mean me! There must be some mistake. I surely couldn't have heard you right." Spencer slowly sat down but missed the chair and sank to the floor! A thousand thoughts rushed through his mind. He still could hardly believe what he had heard. Finally he told President Clark, "I will come to Salt Lake City to talk it over."

The next few days he was in a daze. He and Camilla could not sleep. He prayed almost constantly for six days and nights. He prayed for forgiveness of his weaknesses and imperfections. He prayed for strength to do right. Above all, he prayed that he might feel that he was truly called by the Lord.

Finally on Wednesday, July 14, 1943, he went alone at dawn into the hills. He was fasting. He climbed and climbed, he stumbled on and on to the top of the mountain. He later said, "How I prayed! How I suffered! How I wept! How I struggled!" Then after a long time it seemed a dream came to him. He saw his grandfather, Heber C. Kimball, and thought of his great work and sacrifice. Suddenly, with this dream, came peace, as the quiet after the storm. He knew then, that he *was* called to the work.

For the next thirty years Elder Kimball served as an apostle. When he was assigned to the Church Indian Affairs Committee, he remembered the patriarchal blessing he had received as an eleven-year-old. He was told then that he would have a special teaching mission to the Indians.

THINK ABOUT IT

1. What were some of the Church callings Spencer had in his life? How did he fulfill them?
2. How did Spencer's parents teach him to live the gospel of Jesus Christ?
3. What were some of the trials of President Spencer W. Kimball's life? How did he face them?
4. Tell about Spencer's call to the Quorum of the Twelve Apostles. What did he do before he accepted the call? Why did he do these things?

At the death of President Harold B. Lee, the mantle of the President of the Church and Prophet of God fell unpon Spencer W. Kimball. The date was December 30, 1973, when Spencer was seventy-eight years old. He felt the overwhelming responsibility of the calling, but he knew that God would give him strength, as he always had in the past. One of the apostles said of Spencer, "He believes that the impossible is possible with the help of God. . . ."

His administration was one of exciting changes and accomplishments. He toured the world, visiting the Saints and presiding over area conferences. Through his inspiration, plans were made to build many holy temples throughout the world, and Saints in numerous places across the globe are now enjoying the results of the prophet's vision.

President Kimball was especially known for his talks on repentance, morality, modesty, eternal marriage, and missionary work. He pleaded with the Lord and received a revelation that the priesthood should be available to every worthy male member of the Church.

He gave a personal challenge to all members of the Church: "Lengthen Your Stride!" This has helped the Saints everywhere to pursue excellence and to push themselves to greater efforts in the work of the Lord. President Kimball's energy seemed endless. His motto was, "Do it! Do not delay and put things off. Just do it!" And he was a perfect example of his motto. He expected more of himself than of anyone else. While he asked others to lengthen their stride and quicken their pace, he himself led the way.

46

It was said of him, "Perhaps no one else has been loved so much by so many." Saints throughout the world came to know and love this humble prophet—as they saw him enfold a weeping missionary in his area, hold a crying baby for a mother who was tired and ill, faithfully do his home teaching, help a man in a broken-down car, only asking the man to "say a good word for the Mormons," visit an excommunicated person who was trying to find the way back, or serve his family, Church, members, and the Lord with unequaled love and compassion. His wife said of him, "He is not perfect, but he comes wondrously close!" This is a high tribute from the one who knows him best.

After almost 13 years of dedicated, unwearying service to the Lord and to his children the world over, Spencer Woolley Kimball passed away quietly in his sleep on the evening of November 5, 1985. He was 90 years of age. He was the only prophet many members of the Church, especially younger members and new converts, had ever known. His death was a time of sadness for many people who loved him dearly as their prophet and friend; but it was also a time for many to think about their own lives and how they could follow the example of this great man who had now finished his work on earth and gone to meet his God.

At President Kimball's funeral, President Gordon B. Hinckley paid tribute to him by saying, "On one occasion, I tried to slow him down a little, and he said, 'Gordon, my life is like my shoes—to be worn out in service.'" Truly his life reflected this desire as he shared his great love with friends and strangers alike. Spencer W. Kimball was, in word and deed, a mighty man of God.

TESTIMONY

And then, more than forty years ago, I had a dream, which I am sure was from the Lord. In this dream I was in the presence of my Savior as he stood midair. He spoke no word to me, but my love for him was such that I have not words to explain. I know that no mortal man can love the Lord as I experienced that love from the Savior, unless God reveals it to him. I would have remained in his presence, but there was a power drawing me away from him. And as a result of that dream, I have this feeling—that no matter what might be required at my hands, what the gospel might entail unto me, I would do what I should be asked to do, even to the laying down of my life. And so, when we read in the scriptures what the Savior said to his disciples, "In my Father's house are many mansions. I go to prepare a place for you, that where I am, there ye may be also." I think that is where I want to be. If only I can be with my Savior and have that same sense of love that I had in that dream, it will be the goal of my existence—the desire of my life. Brothers and sisters, I want to add to these testimonies of these prophets my testimony, that I know that he lives and I know that we may see him, and that we may be with him, and that we may enjoy his presence if—that big "if" always—if we will live the commandments of the Lord and do the things which we have been commanded by him to do and reminded by the Brethren to do. And so, I leave this testimony with you in the name of our Lord, Jesus Christ. Amen.